Gary Kasparov's Best Games

Batsford Chess Library

Gary Kasparov's Best Games

International Grandmaster Raymond Keene

An Owl Book
Henry Holt and Company
New York

For Rod, Barbara, and Erin

Henry Holt and Company, Inc.
Publishers since 1866
115 West 18th Street
New York, New York 10011

Henry Holt® is a registered
trademark of Henry Holt and Company, Inc.

First published in the United States in 1993 by
Henry Holt and Company, Inc.
Originally published in Great Britain in 1993 by
B. T. Batsford Ltd.

Library of Congress Catalog Card Number: 93-79187

ISBN 0-8050-3050-6 (An Owl Book: pbk.)

First American Edition—1993

Printed in the United Kingdom
All first editions are printed on acid-free paper.∞

10 9 8 7 6 5 4 3 2 1

Advisor: R. D. Keene, GM, OBE
Technical Editor: Andrew Kinsman

Cover illustration by Brian Robins.

CONTENTS

Algebraic Notation

The moves contained in this book are given in what is known as 'Figurine Algebraic' notation. This describes a very simple and easy way of writing down the moves. Readers familiar with the system can jump ahead to the games themselves, but those who are comparatively new to the game or who have only learned the older 'English Descriptive' notation, will find what follows helpful. It is assumed that the reader already knows how to play chess.

Each piece is represented by a symbol called a 'Figurine', as follows:

	Symbol
Pawn	—
Knight	♘
Bishop	♗
Rook	♖
Queen	♕
King	♔

The squares on the chessboard are described by co-ordinates consisting of a letter followed by a number (see Diagram). For instance, the square marked with a cross is called 'e4'. This follows exactly the same principle as reading off a reference on an A–Z street guide or road map. Everybody can pick this up in a matter of minutes. There is no mystery to it all!

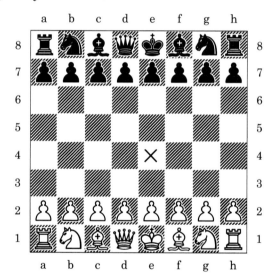

Symbols and abbreviations

+	Check
!	Strong move
!!	Brilliant move
?	Bad move
??	Blunder
!?	Interesting move

INTRODUCTION

Gary Kasparov has always acknowledged two leading influences in his chess career — Alexander Alekhine and Mikhail Botvinnik, two great World Champions. The brilliant games of Alekhine inspired him, but Kasparov has also had the good fortune to have studied personally under Botvinnik in his famous training school. Indeed, it is one of Kasparov's ambitions to establish worldwide branches of the school, to be run by accredited trainers.

Kasparov's rise to World Champion was astoundingly meteoric, although his immense talent was evident from the start. When he was only 11, Botvinnik wrote prophetically: 'The future of chess lies in the hands of this young man.' Kasparov qualified as an International Grandmaster in 1980 at the age of 17, and two years later he was rated as the second strongest player in the world. In November 1985, aged 22, he became the youngest World Champion in the history of the official championship.

From 1984 to 1990, Kasparov played Anatoly Karpov no less than five times for the world title. Kasparov was to speak of Karpov as 'my permanent opponent'. Throughout the course of these difficult encounters, Kasparov displayed an astonishing buoyancy and resilience of spirit.

Gary Kasparov ranks as the greatest player of all time. The January 1990 official FIDE (World Chess Federation) list gave his Elo rating as 2800, the first time a player had ever reached that magic mark and the first time that anyone had bettered Fischer's previous all-time high of 2785. Kasparov was born in Baku (the capital of Azerbaijan) on April 13 1963. His chess talents shone through at an early age and he won the World Junior Championship in 1980. From then onwards, Kasparov tore through the leading ranks of grandmasters like a whirlwind. In 1981 he was equal first with Psakhis in the super-strong USSR Championship and thereafter took a string of clear first places in the strongest tournaments, including Brussels 1986 and Reykjavik 1988. He also played a series of major matches, defeating Beliavsky and Korchnoi in 1983, and Smyslov in 1984 on his way to challenge for the world title.

Kasparov's playing style is that of a self-confident genius who combines the solidity and tenacious defence of Karpov with the fiery brilliance of Tal. Away from the board he is equally formidable in overcoming problems in his path. His disgust with FIDE's handling of the World Championship match in 1984/85 led him to help found the Grandmasters' Association with the intention of giving players a greater influence in the organisation of chess events. In January 1990, during the civil disturbances in Baku, he chartered a plane and dramatically evacuated his wife and other members of his family to safety.

This book details twelve of Kasparov's most brilliant wins, including games against Karpov, England's Nigel Short and the Dutchman, Jan Timman. The latter two fought out the challenge match to decide Kasparov's opponent in the 1993 World Championship final, with Short emerging victorious.

The young Kasparov with his trainers in 1978.

A youthful figure of concentration.

GAME ONE

White: Victor Korchnoi (Switzerland)
Black: Gary Kasparov (USSR)
Lucerne Olympiad 1982
Modern Benoni Defence

For many years I have advocated the following method for young players to improve their results — adopt a personal hero and study that player's games in depth. Such a study will provide a ready-made repertoire and a systematic, coherent method of playing. If your chosen model is still active, this procedure will also furnish a steady flow of combative openings innovations — a vital ingredient of success in modern tournament chess, especially junior chess, where profound study of fashionable openings variations is widely perceived as an infallible key to success.

If a young player's style tends towards the positional or strategic vein, then Petrosian, Botvinnik or Karpov would be the person to choose. If a pupil's inclinations lean towards volatile tactics and ingenious attacking ideas, then the chess teacher should point him (her) in the direction of Alekhine, Tal, Fischer or Spassky.

The clearest example of the latter style, though, is the subject of this book, World Champion Gary Kasparov. His youthfulness makes him a naturally attractive focus for the admiration and attention of young players. He is living proof that the very young can attain the highest pinnacles in chess by sheer force of talent and determination. Kasparov has captured the imagination of chess lovers all over the world through his brilliant victories over Anatoly Karpov in their world title matches and his phenomenal tournament results.

At 22 years of age Gary became the youngest World Champion in the history of the game. His dynamic, sacrificial and revolutionary style of play is certain not only to provide thrills and excitement for those content just to sit back and play over his outstanding games and notes, but it will also furnish red-hot inspiration for everyone who wishes to emulate his style and engage in competitive chess themselves.

The *Financial Times* had this to say of his style: 'While much of modern chess has become dry and technical, Kasparov plays in a way spectators appreciate — he hunts the king with unrestrained ferocity.'

First in this book, a classic attacking game by Kasparov featuring a singular sacrifice of a knight on the e5 square. It was played on a vital occasion for Kasparov, the needle match in the 1982 Olympics, where he faced the then world number two, Victor Korchnoi. At that time Korchnoi was renowned as the most prominent Soviet defector who had twice challenged Anatoly Karpov for the World Championship, while Kasparov was playing on top board in the absence of Karpov, who had taken a day's rest.

1	d4	♞f6
2	c4	g6

Kasparov starts off as if he wants to play the King's Indian Defence.

3	g3	♝g7
4	♝g2	c5

Challenging White in the centre.

5	d5	d6
6	♞c3	0-0
7	♞f3	e6

But now play transposes into the Modern Benoni, an opening ideally suited to Kasparov's uncompromising style.

8	0-0	exd5
9	cxd5	a6 *(1)*

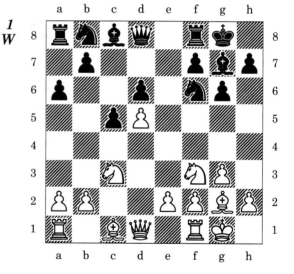

1
W

One of the sharpest variations in modern chess; White has a mobile majority of pawns in the centre, but Black can generate tactical chances both on the queenside and the kingside.

10	a4	♖e8
11	♘d2	♘bd7
12	h3	♖b8
13	♘c4	♘e5
14	♘a3	♘h5
15	e4	♖f8 *(2)*

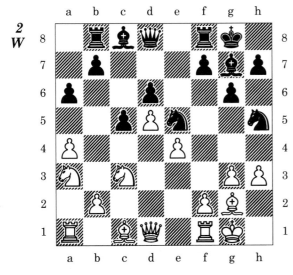

The rook returns in order to lend more punch to the ... f5 thrust.

    16   ♔h2

Safer was 16 ♕e2, discouraging ... b5.

    16   ...   f5
    17   f4

Not 17 exf5 ♗xf5 18 g4? ♗xg4! 19 hxg4 ♕h4+ winning. But now if Black's knight retreats 18 exf5 really is strong. However ...

    17   ...   b5!! *(3)*

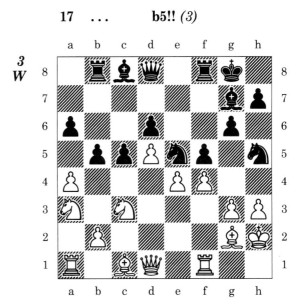

A magnificent conception, whether or not it is completely sound. Black leaves his knight to its fate for seven moves and relies on diversionary tactics.

    18   axb5   axb5
    19   ♘axb5

If 19 fxe5 ♗xe5! threatening both 20 ... b4 and 20 ... ♘xg3, would be very strong.

    19   ...   fxe4
    20   ♗xe4

Now if 20 fxe5 ♗xe5 21 ♗f4 ♘xf4 22 gxf4 ♗xf4+ 23 ♔h1 ♕h4 gives Black a murderous attack.

20	...	♗d7
21	♕e2	♕b6
22	♘a3	♖be8 *(4)*

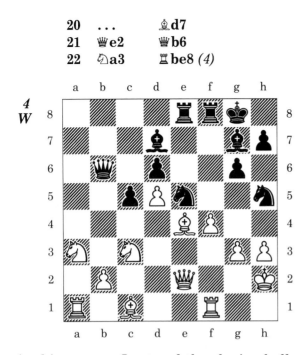

At this moment I entered the playing hall and decided to try to watch the Korchnoi–Kasparov game. Of course, it was impossible to see anything —

hundreds of spectators had crowded around the game and people were even standing on chairs to get a better view. I then glanced up at the manual demonstration board perched above the players' heads and saw the position in the diagram. My immediate reaction was: 'Gary's a pawn down and when he retreats his attacked knight on e5, then White can play the strong ♘c4'. Then I realised it was Korchnoi's move! This is, in fact, the most critical moment. Over to Kasparov himself for his explanation: 'Now what is to be done if Korchnoi takes the knight? After 23 fxe5 one can look into 23 ... ♗xe5 24 ♗f4 ♘xf4 25 gxf4 ♗xf4+! 26 ♔g2 ♕d8 when White has an extra piece but some of them are poorly placed, e.g. the a3-knight, while Black has many advantages on the king's wing.' In fact, Black has full compensation here.

23	♗d2?	♛xb2
24	fxe5	

At last, White accepts the bait — and his position rapidly disintegrates.

24	...	♗xe5
25	♘c4	♘xg3
26	♖xf8+	♖xf8
27	♕e1 (5)	

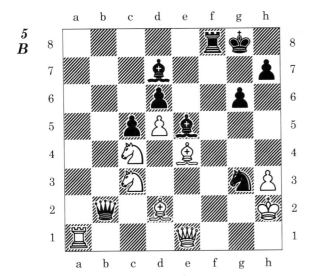

An admission of defeat, but there was no adequate alternative.

27	...	♘xe4+
28	♔g2	♛c2
29	♘xe5	

Or 29 ♖c1 ♛d3 threatening 30 ... ♛xh3+. Now 29 ... ♘xd2 wins.

29	...	♖f2+?

Kasparov: 'This spoils the game and makes the win uncertain. I had prepared for 30 ♔g1 but ...'

30	♕xf2!	♘xf2

The titantic Korchnoi-Kasparov tussle, captured here in its early stages. Looking on is Grandmaster Beliavsky and behind him stands Anatoly Karpov, who had opted for a rest day (Fritz Agterdenbos).

White's queen sacrifice still keeps him fighting on.

31	♖a2!	♛f5!
32	♘xd7	♘d3 (6)

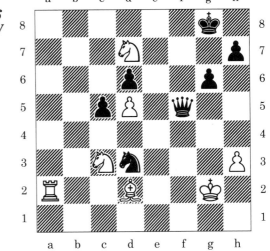

Kasparov: 'After the game I devoted an enormous amount of time to analysing this position. In severe time-trouble Korchnoi played poorly ...'

33	♗h6?

White should play 33 ♖a8+ ♛g7 34 ♖a7! — as Korchnoi pointed out immediately after the game. This still ought to hold the draw.

33	...	♕xd7
34	♖a8+	♔f7
35	♖h8?	♔f6
36	♔f3??	♕xh3+ *(7)*

White lost on time

A magnificent clash; exciting, knife-edge chess. White's 33rd move threw away a possible draw but, on the whole, Kasparov fully deserved to win!

This game was a portent of things to come. In the Candidates' semi-final match between Kasparov and Korchnoi, which took place the following year in London, Kasparov demolished his older opponent by four wins to one, with six draws.

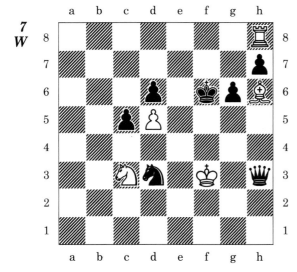

7
W

GAME TWO

White: Gary Kasparov
Black: Anatoly Karpov
World Championship match (48), Moscow 1984/85
Petroff Defence

The first world title clash between the superstars Kasparov and Karpov commenced in Moscow in the autumn of 1984. This match was hailed as a battle between two different Soviet philosophies: Karpov on the one hand, represented conformity to the established regime, while Kasparov had emerged as a constructive critic of the state, eager to forge contacts with the West, and a forerunner of the coming moods of *glasnost* and *perestroika*. The world title was to go to the first to achieve six wins, with no other limit on the duration of the match.

In the first nine games Karpov demonstrated the power and resilience of a true World Champion, notching up four wins and five draws. Game nine from this phase was perhaps the most expertly conducted endgame of all the matches that the two have contested. In 1975, Karpov had taken the world title from Fischer by default and the intervening years had shown that he was, indeed, a worthy successor to the mercurial American. In contrast Kasparov, the young challenger, seemed dispirited and unable to fight back. At the age of 21, he had not yet had sufficient experience in top-level match play to be able to display his tigerish aggression to good effect.

In games 10–26 Kasparov regained his balance, tenaciously holding his opponent to a string of draws, so that Karpov was unable to make a breakthrough until game 27. Now the World Champion was in a commanding position and needed only one more win to retain his title, but he was curiously unable to deliver the death blow. Karpov's play suddenly seemed flaccid and lifeless and there were rumours that he was physically and psychologically drained by the unprecedented length of this marathon match. There followed a sequence of a further 21 games, with 18 draws and 3 wins to Kasparov, the last two wins coming in quick succession in games 47 and 48.

At that point the five-month challenge was unexpectedly terminated by Florencio Campomanes, the President of FIDE (the World Chess Federation) when the score was five to three in Karpov's favour, with no less than 40 draws. At a press conference Campomanes declared that the match had exhausted the participants and ordered that a rematch start in September of the same year, but he was interrupted by the angry interjections of Kasparov, who took the microphone in order to demand that play continue. After a one-hour session with the participants, Campomanes announced that his ruling would stand. However,

Kasparov was to remain bitter about the halt to the proceedings at a point where he had seemingly found his form, and this undoubtedly gave him the extra determination to succeed when the rematch was held in Moscow at the end of 1985.

Here is the historic final game of the aborted 1984 match.

Gary Kasparov and Anatoly Karpov, the greatest rivals in World Championship Chess.

	1	e4	e5
	2	♘f3	♘f6
	3	♘xe5	d6

Not the trap 3 ... ♘xe4?? 4 ♕e2 ♘f6 5 ♘c6+ winning the house.

	4	♘f3	♘xe4
	5	d4	d5
	6	♗d3	♘c6
	7	0-0	♗e7
	8	c4	♘f6

The position looks level, but White still has a slight initiative.

	9	♘c3	0-0
	10	h3 *(8)*	

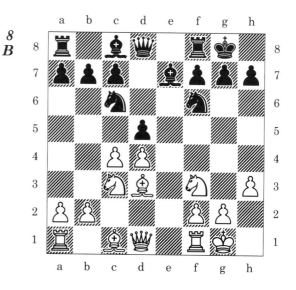

After 10 ♖e1 Black could have played 10 ... ♗g4, equalising comfortably.

10	...	dxc4
11	♗xc4	♘a5
12	♗d3	♗e6
13	♖e1	♘c6

13 ... c5, liquidating the central pawns, would have left White with only a microscopic advantage.

| 14 | a3 |

Preventing 14 ... ♘b4 and 15 ... ♘bd5.

14	...	a6
15	♗f4	♕d7? *(9)*

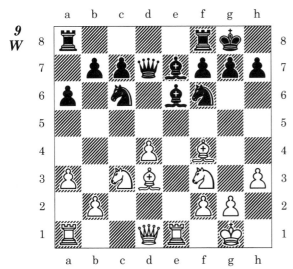

Unnecessarily committing the queen to a square on which she turns out to be exposed; 15 ... ♘d5 preparing ... ♗f6 was preferable.

16	♘e5	♘xe5
17	dxe5	♘d5
18	♘xd5	♗xd5
19	♕c2!	

Surprisingly strong and probably underestimated by Karpov.

| 19 | ... | g6 |

Since this move leads to a clear disadvantage 19 ... h6 was, by a process of elimination, widely suggested as an improvement. However, White obtains a powerful initiative after 19 ... h6 20 ♗f5! ♕c6 21 ♕xc6 ♗xc6 22 e6 menacing the c-pawn; or 20 ... ♕d8 21 ♖ad1 c6 22 e6 with a powerful attack.

20	♖ad1	c6
21	♗h6	♖fd8 *(10)*

| 22 | e6! |

Obvious and strong.

| 22 | ... | fxe6 |

Of course 22 ... ♗xe6 loses to 23 ♗xg6 and after 22 ... ♕e8 23 ♕c3 forces 23 ... f6, leaving White with a pawn wedge on e6. Painful though this would have been for Black, it may have been the lesser evil since after the text Black's weak e-pawn and exposed king offer him very forlorn hopes of survival.

| 23 | ♗xg6 | ♗f8 |

Obviously Black cannot capture the bishop.

24	♗xf8	♖xf8
25	♗e4	♖f7
26	♖e3	♖g7
27	♖1d3	

White is able to feed his pieces into the attack while Black can do little but sit back and nervously await developments.

| 27 | ... | ♖f8 |
| 28 | ♖g3 | |

Threatening 28 ♗xh7+! ♔xh7 (the g7-rook is pinned) 29 ♖xd5+.

28	...	♔h8
29	♕c3	♖f7
38	♖de3 (11)	

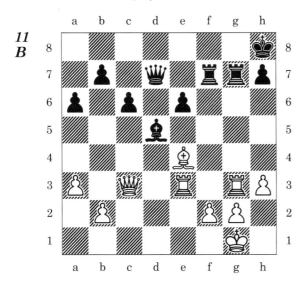

11
B

White's heavy artillery rumbling along the third rank makes an imposing picture.

| 30 | ... | ♔g8 |

If 30 ... ♕c7, to keep White's queen out of e5, 31 ♗xd5 breaks through.

| 31 | ♕e5 | ♕c7? |

This simply loses a pawn. The threat of 32 ♖xg7+ ♖xg7 33 ♕b8+ ♔f7 34 ♖f3+ ♔e7 35 ♕f8+ should have been prevented by 31 ... ♕d8. White can pile on the pressure by e.g. 32 ♖ef3 or an advance of the h-pawn, but Black can fight on.

| 32 | ♖xg7+ | ♖xg7 |
| 33 | ♗xd5 | ♕xe5 |

If 33 ... exd5 34 ♕e8 mate.

| 34 | ♗xe6+ | |

Perhaps Karpov, who was now very short of time, overlooked the X-ray defence of this bishop.

| 34 | ... | ♕xe6 |
| 35 | ♖xe6 (12) | |

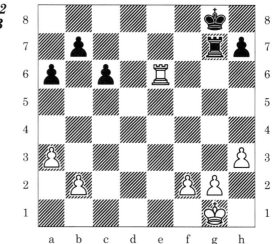

12
B

The smoke has cleared and White is a solid pawn up.

35	...	♖d7
36	b4	♔f7
37	♖e3	♖d1+
38	♔h2	♖c1
39	g4	b5
40	f4	c5
41	bxc5	

This move was sealed as the game was adjourned overnight. As expected, Kasparov now had little difficulty in converting his extra pawn into a win.

41	...	♖xc5
42	♖d3	♔e7
43	♔g3	a5
44	♔f3	b4 (13)

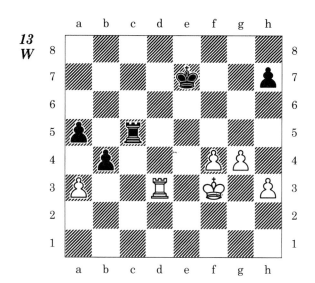

13 W

53	...	♖h1
54	♔d5	♖d1+
55	♖d4	♖e1
56	♔d6	♖e8
57	♔d7	*(14)*

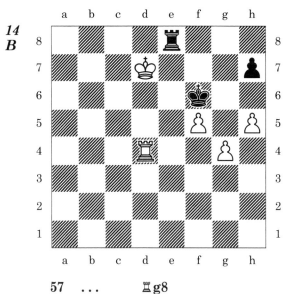

14 B

If Black sits tight, White can gradually advance his kingside pawns. Eventually he will be able to create two united passed pawns which will shelter the king from checks as he shepherds them to greener pastures on the eighth rank. Now, however, the white king just has time to trek over to the queenside and block Black's b-pawn.

45	axb4	axb4
46	♔e4	♖b5
47	♖b3	♖b8
48	♔d5	♔f6
49	♔c5	♖e8
50	♖xb4	♖e3

White had to be sure that Black could not now eliminate sufficient kingside pawns to secure the draw.

| 51 | h4 | ♖h3 |

After 51 ... h5 52 ♖b6+ ♔f7 53 g5 White can sacrifice the h-pawn and rely on the other two.

| 52 | h5 | ♖h4 |
| 53 | f5 | |

The rather ugly configuration of White's pawns does not matter since Black should never be able to capture on g4.

| 57 | ... | ♖g8 |

If the rook stays on the e-file, White can play 58 ♖d6+ answering 58 ... ♔f7 by 59 g5 and 58 ... ♔g5 by 59 ♖e6.

58	h6	♔f7
59	♖c4	♔f6
60	♖e4	♔f7
61	♔d6	

With the black king on f7, White can now answer 61 ... ♖d8+ by 62 ♔e5 followed by ♔f4 and g5. This was the point of White's temporising move 59 ♖c4.

61	...	♔f6
62	♖e6+	♔f7
63	♖e7+	♔f6
64	♖g7!	♖d8+

Of course, 64 ... ♖xg7 65 hxg7 ♔xg7 66 ♔e7, followed by the march of the f-pawn, is hopeless for Black.

65 ♔c5 *(15)*

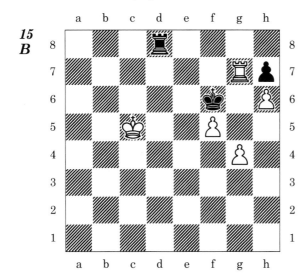

65 ... ♖d5+!

Karpov earns his one exclamation mark of the game for his sportsmanship in providing the spectators with a little fun rather than from any likelihood that Kasparov would actually fall into the stalemate trap.

66 ♔c4   ♖d4+
67 ♔c3   Black resigns

If the rook moves along the d-file White can take the h-pawn and if it stays on the fifth rank to attack the g-pawn, White's king can return to its defence.

Kasparov and Karpov in familiar World Championship pose.

Г.КАСПАРОВ   А.КАРПОВ

GAME THREE

White: Anatoly Karpov
Black: Gary Kasparov
World Championship match (24), Moscow 1985
Sicilian Defence, Scheveningen Variation

The second match between Karpov and Kasparov for the World Championship took place in 1985, and was to consist of 24 games (as would all future championship matches between the two). It was notable that both players were in splendid form, both physically and in terms of the quality of their performance at the board. After a convincing win in game one, Kasparov fell prey to over-confidence, losing games four and five. Thereafter, he went onto the attack, but could not manage to break through the champion's magnificent resistance until game 11, when a powerful queen sacrifice allowed him his second win. Now Kasparov had developed the confidence to fire off theoretical innovations in nearly every game and was repaid with wins in games 16 and 19. However, Karpov took game 22 and needed only one more win to level the score and retain his title. The 23rd game was a draw, leaving everything hanging on the last game of the series. Kasparov won, and in doing so became, at 22, the youngest World Champion in the history of the game.

This was a memorable game — the most important in this book. Karpov launched a vigorous attack against Black's king, but he was then stopped dead in his tracks by an ingenious pawn sacrifice. At first, observers were very confused,but Kasparov had it all worked out, and as Karpov's clock ticked away, the watching grandmasters decided that Black's chances were certainly sufficient for a draw.

Clearly, however, Karpov could not acquiesce in sharing the point, since by doing so he would have forfeited his title to Kasparov. In striving for more, he stumbled into a further sacrifice followed by a blitz counter-offensive and finally the laying-waste of the entire white position during the champion's desperate time-trouble. When Karpov finally conceded defeat, and thereby lost the title he had held for ten years, pandemonium broke out in the playing hall, with frenetic fans chanting and cheering. Protests from frustrated officials that 'this is chess — not football' went unheeded.

The game had been worthy of such a great occasion. It was conducted with immense courage and resource by both players. One top grandmaster remarked: 'It is probably one of the greatest games Kasparov has ever played. His final attack was absolutely brilliant and I hope he can continue to produce such stunning chess for us in the future.' The crowds cheered and stamped, it was an historic moment.

At the moment of victory, when Karpov extended his hand, Kasparov turned towards the audience and, savouring his success, threw his arms in the air. This dramatic gesture was captured in a freeze-frame on that evening's Moscow TV analysis programme. That photo later went the rounds of the world's press.

	1	e4	c5

Requiring only a draw, Kasparov still selects the sharpest possible defence against White's opening move.

2	♘f3	d6
3	d4	cxd4
4	♘xd4	♘f6
5	♘c3	a6
6	♗e2	e6

The so-called Scheveningen variation, a tough line which became Kasparov's favourite and about which he has written the definitive book.

7	0-0	♗e7
8	f4	0-0
9	♔h1	♕c7 *(16)*

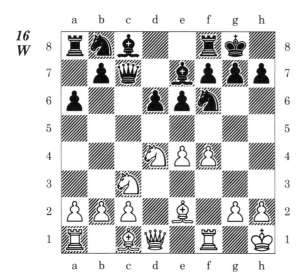

Heralding future counterplay along the half-open c-file.

10	a4	♘c6
11	♗e3	♖e8
12	♗f3	♖b8
13	♕d2	♗d7
14	♘b3	b6
15	g4	

This position had already occurred in the match, but Karpov's 15th move constitutes an aggressive thrust which was a new departure for him. The disadvantage is that this pawn move leaves a vacuum in its wake which may present a future source of weakness.

15	...	♗c8
16	g5	♘d7
17	♕f2 *(17)*	

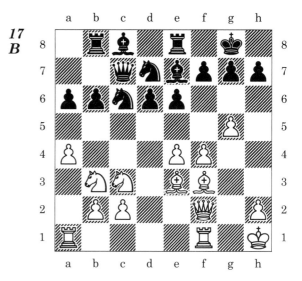

Varying from the game A. Sokolov–Ribli which had just been played at the Montpellier Candidates tournament and had been published in Moscow only two days before this game. There White tried 17 ♗g2 which was met by 17 ... ♘a5. Karpov attempts to improve White's conduct of the attack.

17	...	♗f8
18	♗g2	♗b7
19	♖ad1	g6
20	♗c1	♖bc8

This is not best. Black should play 20 ... ♘c5!

Left to right: Gary Kasparov, ex-British Prime Minister James Callaghan, Anatoly Karpov and FIDE President Florencio Campomanes at the London leg of the 1986 World Championship (Fabio Biagi).

21 ♖d3

Introducing an apparently crude, but nevertheless dangerous, attacking scheme.

21	...	♘b4
22	♖h3	♗g7
23	♗e3?	

White hopes to follow up with ♕h4 and f4–f5, but his slow offensive is hampered by the distance of his knights from the main scene of action. Very dangerous for Black is 23 f5!

23	...	♖e7
24	♔g1	♖ce8! *(18)*

18 W

Kasparov's defence is extremely profound, culminating in this apparently mysterious massing of his rooks in the confined spaces of the closed king's file. The main idea is to discourage White from playing f4–f5 when the answer ... e6xf5 will permit Black's rooks to rampage down the newly opened central file.

25	♖d1	f5

Kasparov breaks out and his rooks soon begin to play their part in his counterattack. The text involves an imaginative sacrifice of his b-pawn.

26	gxf6	♘xf6
27	♖g3	

If immediately 27 ♗xb6, then either 27 ... ♕b8, as in the game, or even 27 ... ♘g4.

27	...	♖f7
28	♗xb6	♕b8
29	♗e3	♘h5
30	♖g4	♘f6
31	♖h4	

Karpov should have retreated with 31 ♖g3, but this would have allowed 31 ...

♘h5, drawing by repetition of moves and giving Kasparov the title. Striving to avoid this disaster, Karpov stumbles into a brilliant new sacrifice, curiously of Black's other knight's pawn.

31   ...   g5!! *(19)*

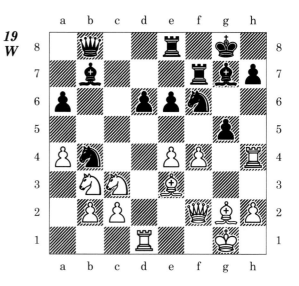

Karpov and Kasparov preparing for action in London (Fabio Biagi).

An unexpected blow that sweeps the remaining shackles from Black's forces. In the last few minutes of play, with the then World Champion in desperate time-trouble, the white position is now utterly routed.

32	fxg5	♘g4
33	♕d2	♘xe3
34	♕xe3	♘xc2
35	♕b6	♗a8
36	♖xd6 *(20)*	

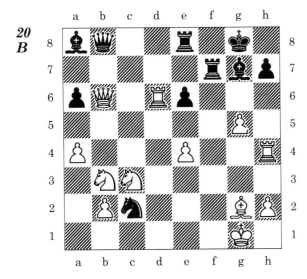

This loses a piece. 36 ♕xb8 ♖xb8 37 ♗h3! was forced.

36	...	♖b7
37	♕xa6	♘xb3

Also rushed for time, Kasparov misses the crushing 37 ... ♘b4!

38	♖xe6	♖xb2
39	♕c4	

Threatening mate on e8, which Kasparov easily sidesteps.

39	...	♔h8
40	e5	♕a7+
41	♔h1	♗xg2+
42	♔xg2	♘d4+ *(21)*

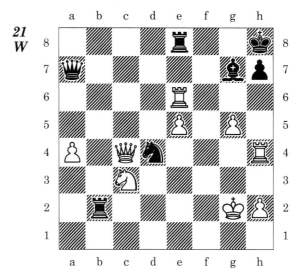

White now resigned the game and the title, making Kasparov the new World Champion.

GAME FOUR

White: Gary Kasparov
Black: Nigel Short
Brussels (OHRA) 1986
Queen's Gambit Declined, Orthodox Variation

Since Karpov was entitled to an immediate return match, the two K's were now scheduled to meet for yet a third time in as many years. The 1986 match commemorated the centenary of the World Championship, which had been inaugurated in 1886 when Steinitz defeated Zukertort in a match that was split between three North American cities. The centenary match echoed this earlier division with the first half being held in London, under the auspices of the GLC, while the second half was played in Leningrad. Kasparov shot into an early lead; by the end of game 16 he had scored 4 wins to Karpov's sole victory. However, Kasparov then suffered a series of losses in games 17 to 19. Many commentators now believed that Kasparov was finished, that, psychologically, he could not recover from such a slough of despond. Inexplicably, Karpov then chose to take one of his permitted time-outs. This was undoubtedly an error of judgement on the part of the former champion. The rest gave Kasparov the chance to reconsider his tactics and he coasted home in the final five games, drawing four and winning one, to retain his title.

Kasparov, having confirmed his world title, was now free to play in tournaments again. The OHRA tournament in Brussels in December 1986 reached category 16 and attained the highest average rating (2636) of any tournament since the international rating system was introduced. Nevertheless, Kasparov won the tournament in crushing style and by a colossal margin. Of the thirty games, twenty were decisive, an incredible quantity for such a top-level clash. Here is Kasparov's revenge for Nigel Short's win against him in the first cycle. This game was, incidentally, awarded the brilliancy prize.

1	d4	e6
2	♘f3	♘f6
3	c4	d5

This opening gives White a slight edge, but Black's position is very hard to break down.

4	♘c3	♗e7
5	♗g5	h6
6	♗xf6	

White decides not to lose time by retreating his bishop and decides to exchange at once.

6	...	♗xf6
7	e3	0-0

8 ♖c1 *(22)*

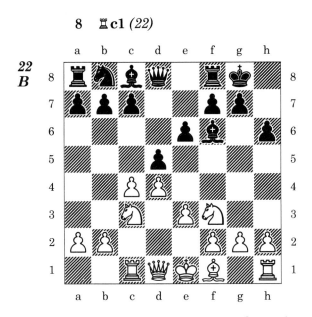

22
B

Kasparov's favourite form of the Queen's Gambit.

8 ... c6

To bolster the centre.

9	♗d3	♞d7
10	0-0	dxc4
11	♗xc4	e5
12	h3	exd4

Inflicting an isolated queen's pawn on White but, in compensation, Kasparov has plenty of activity.

| 13 | exd4 | ♞b6 |
| 14 | ♗b3 | |

The white bishop occupies a particularly powerful diagonal on this square.

Gary Kasparov and Nigel Short in action.

14	...	♗f5
15	♖e1	♗g5 (23)

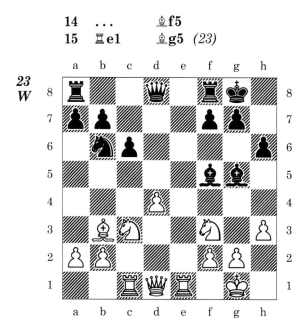

An innovation. After 16 ♘xg5 ♕xg5 White has nothing.

16	♖a1	♘d7

To stop ♘e5.

17	d5	♖c8
18	♘d4	

Inaugurating a cunning manoeuvre.

18	...	♗g6
19	♘e6!! (24)	

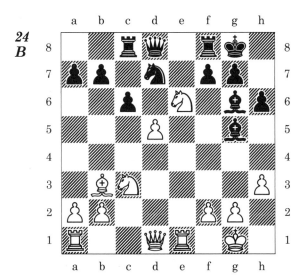

One of those brilliant and surprising tactical coups which have made Kasparov's reputation. Black is forced to accept the sacrifice.

19	...	fxe6
20	dxe6	♔h7

Black cannot retain the extra piece.

21	♕xd7	

If 21 exd7 ♖c7 22 ♗e6 ♗f5! ultimately regains the pawn.

21	...	♕b6
22	e7	♖fe8

If 22 ... ♖xf2? 23 ♘a4! wins or 22 ... ♕xf2+ 23 ♔h1 ♖fe8 24 ♘e4 with great advantage.

23	♕g4	♕c5
24	♘e4	♕xe7
25	♗c2! (25)	

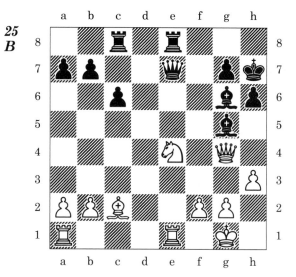

A remarkable position. Black has no useful move and is also threatened with f4 followed by ♘g5+.

25	...	♖f8
26	g3	♕d8
27	♖ad1	♕a5
28	h4	♗e7
29	♘c3!	

The final blow which permits White's rooks to invade the seventh rank.

29	...	♗xc2
30	♖xe7	♖g8
31	♖dd7	♗f5
32	♖xg7+	♔h8
33	♕d4 *(26)*	**Black resigns**

After 33 ... ♗xd7 34 ♖xd7+ mates briskly.

A marvellous game against Kasparov's 1993 World Championship Challenger.

26 B

Gary Kasparov at the 1987 Brussels Swift tournament, where he shared first place with Ljubomir Ljubojevic (Sabine Kaufman).

GAME FIVE

White: Gary Kasparov
Black: Vassily Ivanchuk
USSR Championship, Moscow 1988
English Opening

The fourth Kasparov–Karpov battle for the world title was launched in Seville in October 1987 and Karpov demonstrated early on that he was by no means finished as a championship contender, taking a 3–2 lead in the first five games. Kasparov managed to equalise in game eight but then a series of insipid draws and blundering losses by both players left the score equal at the end of game 22. Kasparov's gaffe in the next game appeared to have cost him the title, but in game 24 he rose magnificently to the occasion. His superb endgame technique converted a complex adjourned position into a win and left Kasparov in possession of the coveted World Championship title for a further three years.

The next year, 1988, Kasparov launched himself into tournament play once again. Kasparov and Karpov dominated what may have been the strongest ever as well as one of the last USSR Championships. The category 14 tournament was held at Moscow's new International Hotel, a complex of shops, restaurants and hotel rooms implemented by the famous internationalist, Dr Armand Hammer.

Kasparov and Karpov were both unbeaten and, for what it is worth, Kasparov came out ahead in the tie-break, though in all-play-all events such splits are artificial. Kasparov's best game was against one of the new aspirants to his title, Vassily Ivanchuk.

1	c4	♘f6
2	♘c3	e5
3	♘f3	♘c6
4	g3	♗b4 (27)

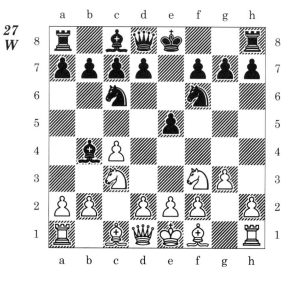

In 1987 Kasparov increasingly turned to the English Opening as one of his main weapons as White. The variation from this game was given a thorough testing, for example, in the World Championship match in Seville. Perhaps Kasparov resorted to the English under the influence of his old mentor, Mikhail Botvinnik, whose favourite it was in his later period.

5	♗g2	0-0
6	0-0	e4
7	♘g5	♗xc3
8	bxc3	♖e8
9	f3 (28)	

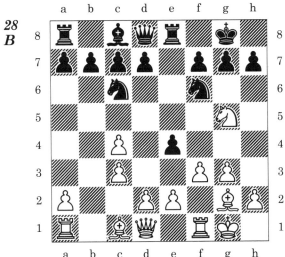

This position arose twice in the 1987 Seville match. In game two Karpov chose 9 ... e3 and won after hideous complications, although subsequent analysis demonstrated that the move was probably dubious.

9	...	exf3
10	♘xf3	d5

This is the old move, approved by theory for years. In game four from Seville, Karpov avoided it with 10 ... ♕e7. Ivanchuk decides that he wants to be shown the theoretical surprise that Kasparov must have had up his sleeve.

11 d4!

An entirely new idea, offering to gambit the pawn on c4 (the previously seen move was 11 cxd5). Kasparov's idea is all the more astonishing in that he not only sacrifices a pawn but also leaves himself with a backward e-pawn on an open file — quite sufficient in itself for masters of the classical mould to have rejected White's concept.

11	...	♘e4

If 11 ... dxc4 12 ♗g5 h6 13 ♗xf6 ♕xf6 14 ♘e5.

12	♕c2	dxc4
13	♖b1	f5
14	g4! (29)	

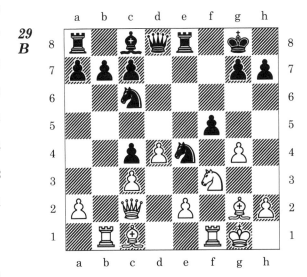

One of the young pretenders, Vassily Ivanchuk (Mark Huba).

A brilliant move, striking at Black's centralised knight by undermining its lateral foundations. If now 14 ... fxg4 15 ♘e5 ♘xe5 16 ♗xe4 ♘c6 17 ♗xh7+ ♔h8 18 ♖b5 threatening the deadly swoop ♖h5. If instead 16 ... ♘g6, then 17 ♗xg6 hxg6 18 ♕xg6 with a fierce attack.

14	...	♕e7
15	gxf5	♘d6

Black's original intention must have been 15 ... ♗xf5, but then 16 ♘e5 leads to complications which favour White. 16 ♘g5 is a complex alternative that Black would also have had to consider.

16	♘g5	♕xe2

Or 16 ... h6 17 ♗d5+ ♔h8 18 f6 gxf6 19 ♖xf6.

17	♗d5+	♔h8
18	♕xe2	♖xe2
19	♗f4	♘d8 (30)

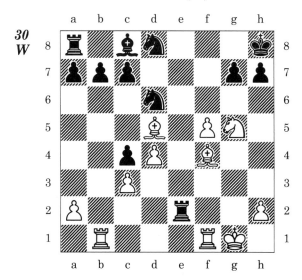

Perhaps 19 ... h6, at long last, would have been a better try. In any case, 19 ... ♗xf5 20 ♗xd6 ♗xb1 21 ♘f7+ ♔g8 22 ♘d8+ is hopeless. Now Kasparov mops up briskly.

20	♗xd6	cxd6
21	♖be1	♖xe1
22	♖xe1	♗d7
23	♖e7	♗c6
24	f6 (31)	Black resigns

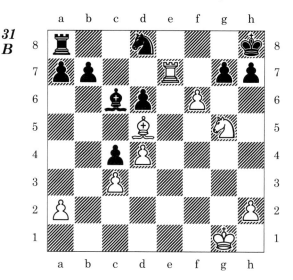

A wonderful blend of efficiency and imagination from the champion.

Gary Kasparov prepares to play Ivanchuk at Dortmund 1992 (Sabine Kaufman).

GAME SIX

White: Gary Kasparov
Black: Valery Salov
World Cup, Barcelona 1989
English Opening

A prestigious new event in the world chess calendar was the World Cup series, and Kasparov won this with consummate ease. It was remarkable that in four exceptionally powerful tournaments in France, Iceland, Spain and Sweden, he lost just three games.

In the Barcelona World Cup Kasparov began with all the alacrity of a snail on tranquillisers. In his second game he lost to Artur Yusupov, while his score was also littered with lacklustre draws against Ribli, Seirawan and Hübner. But as time ran out in his race against Ljubojevic for first prize, the champion finally picked up momentum.

1	♘f3	♘f6
2	c4	b6
3	♘c3	c5
4	e4	d6

Valery Salov, joint winner (with Nigel Short) of the powerful Amsterdam tournament in 1991, ahead of both Kasparov and Karpov (Mark Huba).

Apparently, a slow flank opening, but given the dynamic Kasparov treatment, it soon turns into a sacrificial orgy of attack.

5	d4	cxd4
6	♘xd4	♗b7
7	♕e2	♘bd7 (32)

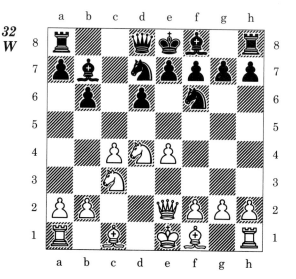

Black's formation is known as the 'Hedgehog' and is meant, in theory, to be impervious to attack.

8	g3	♖c8
9	♗g2	a6
10	0-0	♕c7
11	b3	e6

The move order of the opening has been somewhat unusual, but given a couple more moves such as ... ♗e7 and ... 0-0, Black will transpose into his normal Hedgehog system. Kasparov, however, does not grant this respite and launches an immediate attack.

12 ♘d5! *(33)*

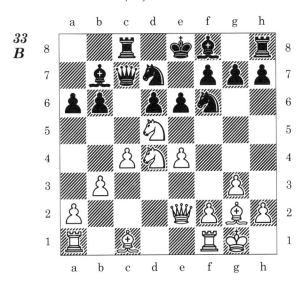

A brilliant and powerful sacrifice.

12 ... ♕b8

If 12 ... exd5 13 exd5+ ♔d8 14 ♖e1 with a fearsome onslaught.

13	♖d1	g6
14	♗g5	♗g7
15	♗xf6	♘xf6
16	♘xb6	♖d8

Kasparov has won a pawn, but he is not content with that. Although he could now simply consolidate with 17 ♘a4, Black could then escape the worst with 17 ... 0-0 and ... ♖fe8. Kasparov prefers to blast his hapless opponent from the face of the board with a veritable banquet of further sacrifices.

17	e5	♗xg2
18	exf6	♗xf6
19	♘xe6!	*(34)*

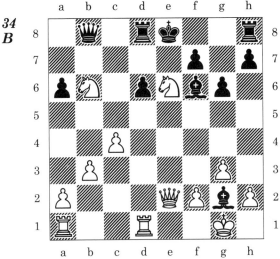

Hammer blow after hammer blow.

19	...	fxe6
20	♕xe6+	♗e7
21	c5	♗b7

Kasparov eyes up Karpov at the 1987 Brussels SWIFT event (Sabine Kaufman).

Black is given no respite.

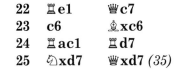

22	♖e1	♛c7
23	c6	♝xc6
24	♖ac1	♖d7
25	♘xd7	♛xd7 (35)

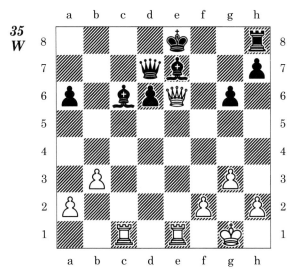

Salov was now banking on 26 ♖xc6 ♛xe6 27 ♖xe6 ♔d7, but instead of allowing Black to return from the grave in this fashion, Kasparov finishes him off with a series of massive punches.

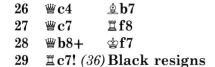

26	♛c4	♝b7
27	♛c7	♖f8
28	♛b8+	♔f7
29	♖c7! (36)	**Black resigns**

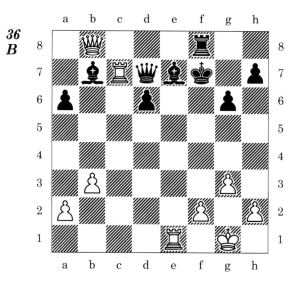

He faces ruinous material losses. A wonderful game.

GAME SEVEN

White: Gary Kasparov
Black: Boris Spassky
Linares 1990
Nimzo-Indian Defence

In October 1989, Gary Kasparov won the category 16 tournament in the Dutch town of Tilburg with the astounding score of 12 points from 14 games. He won 10 games, conceding draws against Korchnoi, Ljubojevic, Sax and Ivanchuk only in those games in which he had to play with the black pieces against them. Kasparov did not just beat his distinguished opponents, he crushed them, not needing to adjourn a single game in the course of his triumph.

This tournament result by the World Champion at once entered the mythology of chess, taking its place alongside such other legendary achievements as Lasker's at St Petersburg 1914, Capablanca's at New York 1927, or Alekhine's at Bled 1931. What is more important, however, than the score itself, is the fact that this performance enabled Kasparov to shatter Bobby Fischer's Elo rating record of 2785, which had previously been considered quite unassailable. The psychological barrier posed by Fischer had now been well and truly swept away. Kasparov consolidated this achievement with a further sensational result at Belgrade in November 1989, which brought his rating up to 2800 at the start of 1990, so he went into the super-strong Linares tournament in February with an air of invincibility.

Boris Spassky, who won the World Championship in 1969, is one of the immortals of chess, having not only reached the pinnacle of world chess, but also twice clashed with Bobby Fischer in memorable matches, twenty years apart. In his prime, his games were as impressive as his results, his opponents often being bowled over by sacrificial attacks, the depths of which they could not fully comprehend. Nowadays, Spassky is more often to be seen consolidating cautiously towards a draw, rather than permitting the full range of his imagination to flow in cavalier attacks. A recent notable exception was the following game where, facing the World Champion with his new rating of 2800, Spassky sought to recapture the glories of his youth. Before this game, Spassky was one of the few grandmasters to enjoy a plus score against Kasparov.

1	d4	♘f6
2	c4	e6
3	♘c3	♗b4
4	♕c2	

Capablanca's variation.

4	...	d5
5	cxd5	exd5
6	♗g5	h6
7	♗h4	c5
8	dxc5!	*(37)*

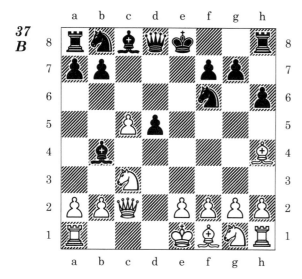

37
B

Kasparov's novel concept, which he had already used to defeat Victor Korchnoi at Tilburg the previous year.

8	...	♘c6

In their post-mortem analysis, the players examined the complex alternative, 8 ... d4 9 0-0-0 g5 10 ♗g3 ♕a5 11 ♖xd4 ♘c6 12 ♖d6 ♔e7 13 ♘f3 ♗e6 14 e3 ♗xc5 15 ♖xe6+, where White sacrifices the exchange in order to expose the black king.

9	e3	g5
10	♗g3	♘e4
11	♘f3	♕f6

Spassky places his hopes on a fierce counterattack against the pinned white knight on c3.

12	♗b5	*(38)*

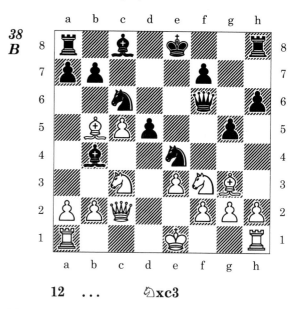

38
B

12	...	♘xc3

Black accepts the challenge and tries to win material by utilising his pressure against White's knight on c3. If now 12 ... ♗f5, then 13 ♗xc6+ bxc6 14 ♗e5 ♘xc3 15 bxc3.

13	♗xc6+	bxc6
14	a3	

The cunning point of White's play, which undermines the influence of Black's dangerous bishop. Of course, 14 bxc3 would be worse than useless after 14 ... ♗xc3+ followed by ... ♗xa1.

14	...	g4

After long thought, which resulted in Black having consumed an hour's thinking time more than his opponent. Spassky, in the style of his youth, decides to sacrifice material to launch a virulent counterattack. Indeed, the other options, 14 ... ♗a5 15 ♗e5 ♘e4+ 16 b4 or 14 ... ♗f5 15 ♕d2 ♗a5 16 ♗e5, were less than appetising.

15	♗e5	♘e4+
16	axb4	♕f5
17	♗xh8	gxf3

18 ♖g1 *(39)*

Kasparov prepares to do battle with Boris Spassky in Linares (Enrique Alonso).

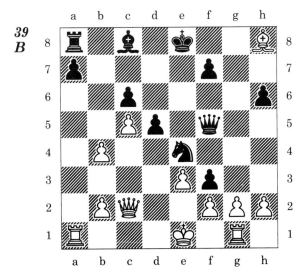

Kasparov has to proceed with the utmost caution. Although he has won rook for knight, his bishop on h8 is in distinct danger of becoming incarcerated.

18 ... ♛g4

In this finely contested battle, the older man finally goes astray and misses a chance to demonstrate that he has real compensation for his sacrifice. The text certainly looks promising, but Spassky had doubtless underestimated the defensive energy which could be generated by the retreat of White's queen on move 19. The correct course would have been 18 ... fxg2 19 ♛e2 and now either 19 ... ♞g5 20 f4 ♞e4, with a light-square blockade, or even 19 ... ♛h3 20 f3 ♛h4+ 21 ♔d1 ♗h3, when White cannot play 22 fxe4 on account of 22 ... ♗g4, netting the white queen. In both cases, Black's prospects would still have been alive. Now, however, Kasparov transforms the situation to his advantage with a few swift, decisive strokes.

19	♕d1	♘g5
20	♕d4	♘e4
21	♕e5+	♗e6
22	♕f4 (40)	

Black's error on move 18 has resulted in two wasted moves with his knight, while White's queen has suddenly assumed a dominating post in the centre of the battlefield.

22	...	♕g6
23	♕xf3	f6

Black's final chance is to trap the white bishop which is stranded on h8.

24	♕f4	♔f7
25	f3	♘g5
26	♔d2	

Connecting his rooks and preventing the immediate capture of the white bishop by 26 ... ♖xh8 on account of 27 ♖xa7+ ♔f8 28 ♕d6+ or 27 ... ♔e8 28 ♕b8+.

26	...	♕f5
27	h4	♕xf4
28	exf4	♘h7
29	g4 (41)	Black resigns

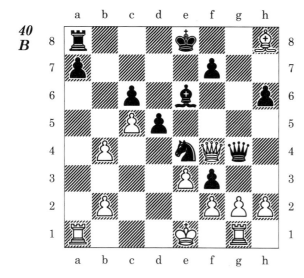

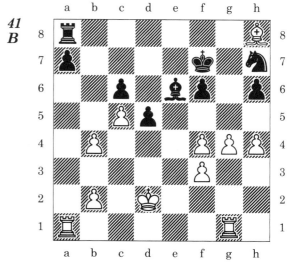

Former World Champion Boris Spassky, who lost his title against the legendary Bobby Fischer at Reykjavik in 1972 (Mark Huba).

Ironically, just at the moment when Black is on the verge of capturing the white bishop, he has to recognise the utter hopelessness of his situation. If 29 ... ♖xh8 30 ♖xa7+ ♔g8 31 f5 ♗f7 32 ♖e1 ♔g7 33 ♖1e7 ♖f8 34 b5 cxb5 35 c6 and Black is paralysed, while White's c-pawn marches on to coronation. A symbolic clash between two generations.

GAME EIGHT

White: Gary Kasparov
Black: Anatoly Karpov
World Championship (20) Lyons 1990
Ruy Lopez, Zaitsev Variation

Having conclusively reinforced his position at the top of the chess world with a string of outstanding tournament victories, Kasparov again faced Karpov for the World Championship in the autumn of 1990. The closeness of this fifth encounter is shown by the final result of Kasparov 12½ points; Karpov 11½. The match, which lasted three months and began in New York before moving to Lyons, produced some of the finest chess between these two players who so towered above all of their contemporary grandmasters. Although there were blunders due to the tenseness of the occasion, many of the games of this latest match will enter the record books as classics.

The 20th game was widely considered to have been the most brilliant in the 1990 World Championship match. Its incredibly high standard shows just how far the rest of the world's grandmasters will have to go if they are to usurp the Russians at the summit of world chess. Kasparov played in his most dramatic style. He showered sacrifices on the black position, first a pawn, then a knight and a bishop. Finally, to eradicate Karpov's remaining resistance, he sacrificed his queen on the 34th move; queen sacrifices at this level of play are rare and highly prized.

This game will become one of the masterpieces to rank with those such as Anderssen's win against Kieseritsky in London in 1851, or Botvinnik's win against Capablanca in Rotterdam in 1938. Unlike great attacking players of the past, however, Kasparov's position during his offensives is often exposed in some other part of the battlefield. Thus, in this game, a black pawn penetrated to the seventh rank, eating white pieces as it went, and for the last 15 moves of the game was just one square away from becoming a queen. The element of extreme danger to himself is what characterises Kasparov's attacking strategy and differentiates it from that of previous World Champions.

The start of this game was a duplicate of game four from this match until Kasparov deviated with a new idea on the 18th move. On the 23rd move he sacrificed a pawn in order to aim his pieces directly at the black king and on move 26 Kasparov sacrificed a knight to strip away the black king's defences, but Karpov would have lost instantly had he accepted the sacrifice. Instead, the former World Champion lunged at a white bishop on the opposite side of the board. On the 29th move Kasparov had virtually every piece lined up against the black king and it was his queen sacrifice on the 34th move that will ensure this game's place in the history of chess. For the last ten moves of the game, Karpov's problems on the board were compounded by a desperate shortage of time. When he resigned on the 41st move he had to reach over and take his opponent's written record of the game to reconstruct his own scoresheet.

1	e4	e5
2	♘f3	♘c6
3	♗b5	a6

This opening, known since the sixteenth century, is named after the Spanish priest and theoretician, Ruy Lopez.

4	♗a4	♘f6
5	0-0	♗e7
6	♖e1	b5
7	♗b3	d6

Looking relaxed at the start of a game in the Lyons leg of the 1990 World Championship match (Sabine Kaufman).

White has attacking chances, but Black's position is resilient.

8	c3	0-0
9	h3	♗b7

10 d4 ♖e8 *(42)*   **19 ♘h2 *(43)***

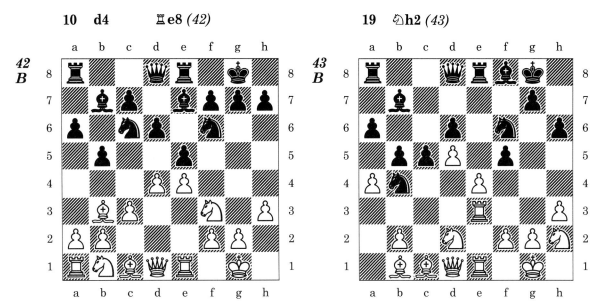

This is all well-known opening theory, contested many times in games between Kasparov and Karpov.

11	♘bd2	♗f8
12	a4	h6
13	♗c2	exd4
14	cxd4	♘b4
15	♗b1	c5

Challenging White in the centre.

16	d5	♘d7
17	♖a3	

A fascinating way of introducing the white queen's rook into a kingside attack.

17	...	f5
18	♖ae3	♘f6

A theoretical novelty which set Karpov thinking. Just as an illustration of how dangerous it is to snatch the central pawn, here is one variation: 19 ... fxe4 20 ♘xe4 ♘bxd5 21 ♘xf6+ ♘xf6 22 ♖xe8 ♘xe8 23 ♕d3 ♘f6 24 ♘g4 with a dreadful attack since White is going to penetrate with his queen to h7. I never tire of stressing in this and cognate variations of the Ruy Lopez, that if White can succeed in blasting open a path for his king's bishop, he will often win.

19	...	♔h8
20	b3	bxa4
21	bxa4	c4
22	♗b2	fxe4
23	♘xe4	♘fxd5
24	♖g3	♖e6
25	♘g4	♕e8

After the game Kasparov said that Karpov had to play 24 ... ♘d3 to stem the flow of White's attack. However, Karpov was doubtless thinking only of victory, having faith in the defensive capacity of his kingside and not wishing to surrender one of his two central passed pawns.

26 ♘xh6!! (44)

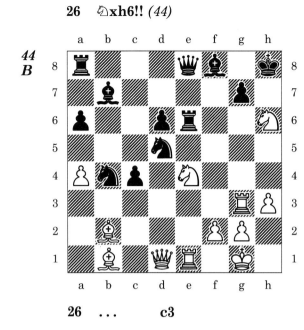

44 B

26 ... c3

The best form of defence is counterattack! After this move it is difficult to believe that White has enough for his sacrificed piece since so much of his army is hanging. Indeed, it is one of the hallmarks of Kasparov's attacks, distinguishing them from those of all of his great predecessors such as Alekhine, Tal, Spassky et al, that when he sacrifices material to launch an offensive, there is often a tremendous element of danger to himself in a completely different part of the board. Thus, here, for example, White is not only a piece down, but Black gets a passed pawn on the seventh rank. One false move in the conduct of the attack will spell certain doom for White.

27	♘f5	cxb2
28	♕g4	♗c8
29	♕h4+	♖h6
30	♘xh6	gxh6

31 ♔h2 (45)

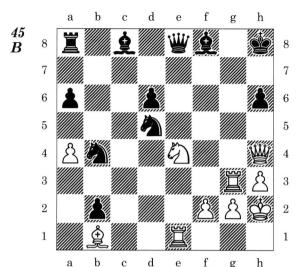

45 B

Typical Kasparov, tucking his king away from annoying checks and thus liberating his rook on e1 for future action. Karpov now had to play the remainder of his moves up to move 40 in a mere three minutes. Given the appalling complexity of the situation from his point of view, it is a tribute to his reflexes that he made the time-control at all.

31	...	♕e5
32	♘g5	♕f6
33	♖e8	♗f5
34	♕xh6+	(46)

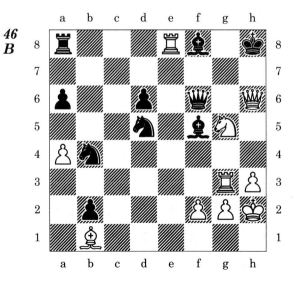

46 B

This position went round the world. It is incredibly unusual to have a queen sacrifice at this level of play, even just a temporary one. In fact, the diagram for this position even made it to the front page of *The Times* for the following day.

34	...	♛xh6
35	♘f7+	♚h7
36	♗xf5+	(47)

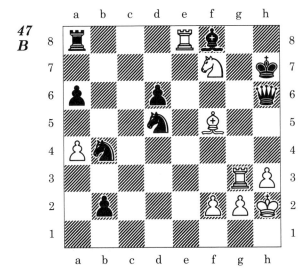

Now all is clear — White wins a mass of material.

36	...	♛g6
37	♗xg6+	♚g7
38	♖xa8	♗e7
39	♖b8	a5
40	♗e4+	♚xf7
41	♗xd5+	Black resigns

A stunning game.

The euphoria of victory in the eighteenth game of the match (Sabine Kaufman).

45

GAME NINE

White: Gary Kasparov
Black: Viswanathan Anand
Tilburg (Interpolis) 1991
Sicilian Defence, Paulsen Variation

It is an interesting fact that for much of the past decade, the majority of Gary Kasparov's opening weaponry has been directed towards his marathon duels with Anatoly Karpov. From 1984 to 1987, Kasparov and Karpov played four World Championship matches, comprising 120 championship games. This works out at about one game every one and a half weeks between the two. Recently, however, the hectic pace of World Championship matches has calmed down. Kasparov has, therefore, been able to broaden his arsenal to include a wider range of exciting and deeply analysed systems to counter the more extensive selection of opponents that he has been facing. One such system is introduced by this game against the young Indian star, Viswanathan Anand, who may well be his challenger in 1996.

1	e4	c5
2	♘f3	♘c6
3	d4	cxd4
4	♘xd4	♕c7
5	♘c3	e6

A flexible and solid set-up known as the Paulsen system.

6 ♗e3 *(48)*

A good alternative is 6 ♗e2, and if Black tries rigorously to stay in the contours of the Paulsen system with 6 ... a6 7 0-0 b5 then 8 ♘xc6 ♕xc6 9 ♗f3 ♗b7 10 ♗f4 d6 11 ♖e1 e5 and now the sacrifice 12 a4!! gives White a tremendous initiative.

6	...	a6
7	♗d3	♘f6
8	0-0	♘e5

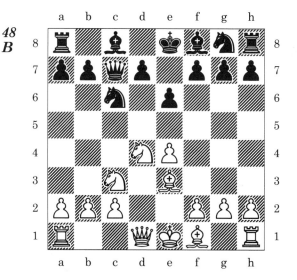

A simplifying strategy at this point would be more prudent than the complicated text move, although White retains a nagging plus after 8 ... ♘xd4 9 ♗xd4 ♗c5 10 ♗xc5.

9 h3 ♗c5

10	♔h1	d6
11	f4	♞c6?

Understandably, Anand underestimates or overlooks the force of White's cunning combination. True, 11 ... ♞xd3 12 cxd3 followed by ♖c1 would negate all of Black's play on the c-file. However, there are two possibly superior alternatives, namely, 11 ... ♞ed7 12 ♕f3 b5 or 11 ... ♞g6 12 ♕f3 0-0 13 ♖ae1 b5 14 f5 ♞e5 15 ♕g3 ♔h8.

12 e5!! (49)

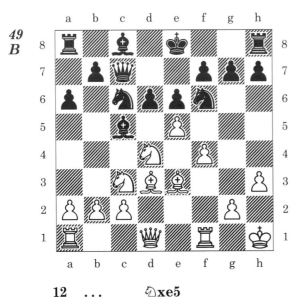

12 ... ♞xe5

Realising his plight, Anand temporarily sacrifices a piece in order to exploit the pin against White's queen's bishop. If instead 12 ... dxe5 13 ♞db5 axb5 14 ♗xc5; 12 ... ♞xd4 13 exf6 gxf6 14 ♞e4 f5 15 ♞xc5 dxc5 16 c3 ♞b5 17 a4; or finally, 12 ... ♗xd4 13 ♗xd4 dxe5 14 fxe5 ♞d7 15 ♞e4 ♞cxe5 16 ♕h5.

13 fxe5 dxe5

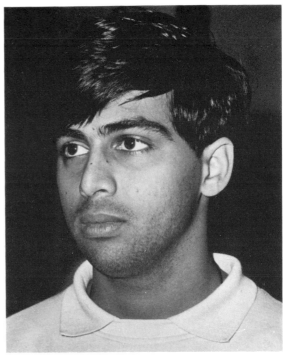

The talented Indian star Viswanathan Anand, who many predict will be a future World Champion (Mark Huba).

14 ♗b5+! (50)

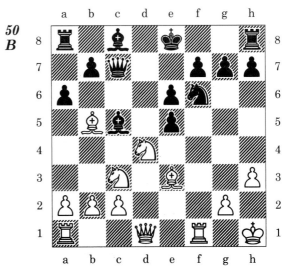

This violent check frustrates Black's plans. White gives back the piece but nails down the black king in the centre.

14 ...   axb5

If 14 ... ♔e7 15 ♖xf6 exd4 16 ♗f4 ♕a5 17 ♕h5 axb5 18 ♖xf7+ and wins.

15	♘dxb5	♕c6
16	♗xc5	♕xc5
17	♘d6+	♔e7
18	♖xf6	gxf6

Black is allowed no respite from White's tempest of an attack. Now 18 ... ♔xf6 is prohibited by a knight check on e4, forking Black's king and queen.

19	♘ce4	♕d4
20	♕h5	♖f8
21	♖d1	♕e3
22	♕h4	♕f4
23	♕e1 (51)	

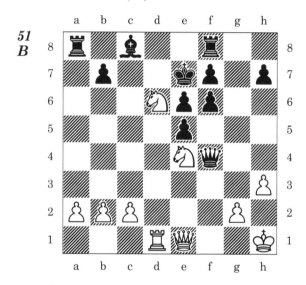

51 B

One of the most attractive attacking motifs in chess. Having concentrated the attack in such a sustained fashion, directly against the black king, this switchback by the white queen rapidly brings about a decision on the other side of the board.

23	...	♖a4
24	♕c3	♖d4
25	♖xd4	♕f1+
26	♔h2	exd4
27	♕c5	♔d7
28	♘b5	♕f4+
29	g3 (52)	**Black resigns**

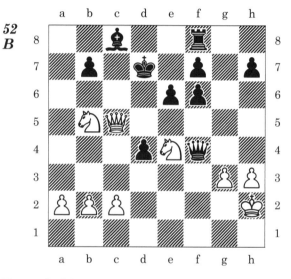

52 B

Remarkably, Kasparov took a mere 40 minutes to play the whole game.

Kasparov and Anand analysing after their second game at Tilburg 1991, in which Anand managed to extract revenge for the featured game (Alain Fayard).

48

GAME TEN

White: Jan Timman
Black: Gary Kasparov
Linares 1992
King's Indian Defence

The great tournament in Linares in February 1992 was undoubtedly one of the very strongest in the entire history of chess, and ended in a superb triumph for the World Champion, who finished a clear two points ahead of the field and was the only unbeaten player. Over the previous year, Kasparov's form had been somewhat uncertain, with just one first prize at Tilburg, and three other events, Linares 1991, Amsterdam in the summer and Reggio Emilia over the new year period, in which the champion was squeezed out of the lead, albeit by half a point in each case. Linares 1992 saw Kasparov restore his reputation, in particular against the four world semi-final aspirants (Karpov, Yusupov, Short and Timman) whom he swept away by the score of 4–0. This must have been a particularly satisfying aspect of his overall victory for Kasparov.

In the next two games we look at two of Kasparov's wins from the Linares tournament. The very first round was a dramatic victory with his favourite King's Indian Defence. Jan Timman, the Dutch Grandmaster, has been one of the world's consistently outstanding players over the last two decades and has been a Candidate for Kasparov's crown on numerous occasions.

1	d4	♞f6
2	c4	g6
3	♞c3	♝g7

Kasparov's favourite counterattacking King's Indian Defence.

4	e4	d6
5	f3	0-0
6	♝e3	e5

The so-called Sämisch variation. White sets up a giant wall of pawns to hem Black in.

7	d5	♞h5
8	♛d2	f5
9	0-0-0	(53)

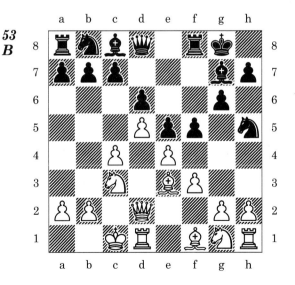

53
B

Positions where the players castle on opposite wings are often characterised by desperate and savage attacks against the opposing king.

| | 9 | ... | ♘d7 |
| | 10 | ♗d3 | ♘c5 |

This is Kasparov's innovation. Conventionally the knight would be regarded as prone to attack on this square; the normal move being 10 ... ♘df6.

| | 11 | ♗c2 | a6 |
| | 12 | ♘ge2 | b5 |

Kasparov is the first to set his attack in motion.

| | 13 | b4 |

Gaining space but also weakening the squares around his king.

	13	...	♘d7
	14	cxb5	axb5
	15	♘xb5	*(54)*

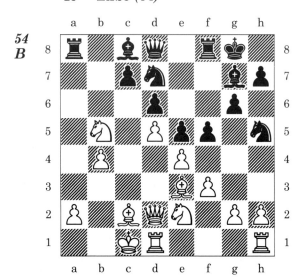

This looks risky since Black's rook can penetrate the white camp, but Timman hopes to drive back the black forces and exploit his control of the queenside light squares.

	15	...	♖xa2
	16	♘ec3	♖a8
	17	♔b2	♘df6
	18	♘a7	fxe4
	19	♘c6	♕d7
	20	g4

Timman overreaches in trying to achieve complete domination of the board by a grandiose attacking scheme. He has overlooked some diabolical tactics and should have contented himself with the humble 20 fxe4.

| | 20 | ... | ♘f4 |
| | 21 | g5 | *(55)* |

The Dutchman Jan Timman, who has been one of the leading players over the last twenty years (Mark Huba).

Were Black now obliged to play 21 ... ♞6h5 then 22 ♗xe4 would in fact cement White's light-squared hegemony over the entire board. With the move ♖a1 in the offing to secure the a-file, Timman would have been able to look forward to the future with confidence. Instead of falling in with this supine course, Kasparov sets the board alight with a sacrifice.

21   ...   ♞6xd5!!
22   ♞xd5

Of course, not now 22 ... ♛xc6 23 ♞e7+ winning for White.

22   ...   ♞d3+ *(56)*

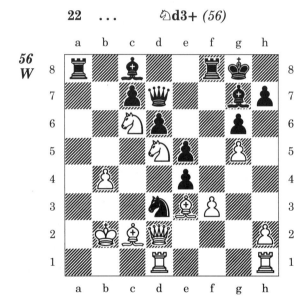

23   ♗xd3

If 23 ♔b3 ♗b7 either wins back material or leads to a mating attack, e.g. 24 b5 ♗xc6 25 bxc6 ♖fb8+. Another possibility is the spectacular queen sacrifice 23 ♔b3 ♛xc6 24 ♞e7+ ♔h8 25 ♞xc6 ♗e6+ 26 ♔c3 ♖a3+ 27 ♗b3 ♖xb3+ 28 ♔c2 ♖b2+ 29 ♔c3 ♖xd2 followed by ... ♖xf3 when Black's central pawns should guarantee victory. However, by playing 23 ♔b1 White could still put Black's idea to the test.

23   ...   exd3
24   ♞ce7+   ♔h8
25   ♞xc8   e4+ *(57)*

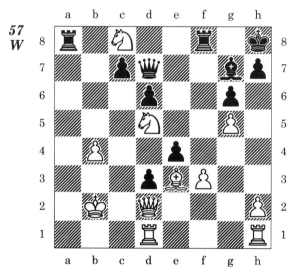

White resigns

After 26 ♔b3 ♛a4+ 27 ♔c4 ♛c6+ 28 ♔b3 ♛xd5 is checkmate; or 26 ♞c3 ♛a4 27 ♔c1 ♛a1+ 28 ♞b1 ♖a2 and Black wins; or finally 26 ♞f6 ♖xf6 27 ♗d4 ♖xf3 28 ♗xg7 ♛xg7+ and Black wins again.

Kasparov carries 'risk' strategy to the maximum, even against his most serious rivals.

*Kasparov and Timman analysing at the
London Docklands match in 1984.*

GAME ELEVEN

White: Gary Kasparov
Black: Nigel Short
Linares 1992
Scotch Game

In Kasparov's victory at Tilburg the previous autumn his closest rival had been Britain's Nigel Short. Short finished ahead of Anand, Karpov, Timman and several other leading grandmasters in Tilburg, firmly establishing himself as a serious contender to Kasparov's crown after his Candidates quarter-final victory over Boris Gelfand only a couple of months before. But at Linares Short was ruthlessly outclassed by the rampant champion.

1	e4	e5
2	♘f3	♘c6
3	d4	exd4
4	♘xd4	♗c5
5	♗e3	♛f6 *(58)*

Kasparov has wheeled out his favourite replacement for the Ruy Lopez, the Scotch Game. This ancient opening was reintroduced to grandmaster practice by Kasparov himself, who used it to great effect in several games during his 1990 World Championship match.

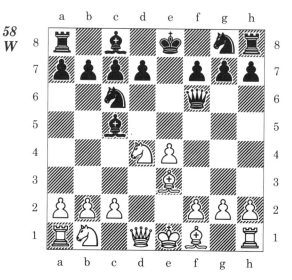

The German grandmaster Robert Hübner against Gary Kasparov at Dortmund 1992 (Helmut Schneider).

GM   ELO   2615
Robert Hübner
Deutschland

GM   ELO   2780
Garri Kasparow
Russland

6	c3	♞ge7
7	♝c4	0-0
8	0-0	♝b6
9	♞c2	d6
10	♝xb6	axb6
11	f4 (59)	

As so often, Kasparov ferries his pieces over towards his opponent's king.

17	...	♝c6
18	♞e3	♞d7 (60)

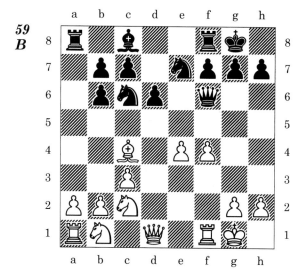

*59
B*

As a result of the opening White enjoys more space, and Nigel tries to break this grip by radical means.

11 ... g5

A controversial concept. Black gains control of the dark squares, but undermines his own defences. In particular, his king may become open to attack later in the game.

12	f5	♞e5
13	♝e2	♝d7
14	c4	g4

A rash advance which runs counter to his previous strategy and positively invites a white sacrifice on g4. Correct was the subtle 14 ... ♝a4.

15	♞c3	h5
16	♛d2	♚h8
17	♛f4	

*60
W*

19 ♝xg4

The long-awaited sacrifice.

19	...	hxg4
20	♞xg4	♛h4
21	♖f3	♞g6

An ingenious defence, for if 22 fxg6 fxg6 and White's attack grinds to a halt.

22	♛e3	♛xg4
23	♛h6+	♚g8 (61)

*61
W*

56

| 24 | ♖h3 |

A slip which prolongs the game without affecting the final outcome. Correct is 24 ♖g3 ♛xg3 25 hxg3 and, if necessary, White will soon decide the game by means of ♔f2 and ♖h1.

24	...	♛xh3
25	gxh3	♘ge5
26	f6	

Forcing the gain of more material.

26	...	♘xf6
27	♛xf6	♖ae8
28	♔h1	♘g6
29	h4	♖e6

White has a tactical win, but there are still obstacles to be overcome in converting the full point.

30	♛g5	♖fe8
31	h5	♖e5
32	♛h6 (62)	

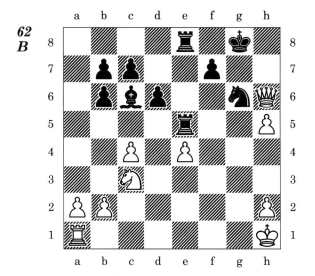

62
B

Once again, White's queen looms into the proximity of Black's king.

32	...	♖xe4
33	♘xe4	♖xe4
34	♔g1	♘e5
35	♛g5+	♔h7
36	♛f5+	♔h6

Black's king looks horribly exposed, but there is no way to nail down the coffin.

37	♖f1	♖e2
38	♛f6+	♔h7
39	♛g5	♗e4
40	h6	♗g6
41	h4 (63)	

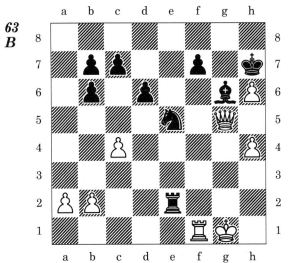

63
B

As played, Kasparov has maintained a fairly easily winning position, but he has had to clinch matters by weight of material advantage rather than by a mating attack. The advance of White's second h-pawn is decisive.

41	...	♖e4
42	h5	♖g4+
43	♛xg4	♘xg4
44	hxg6+	fxg6
45	♖f7+	♔xh6
46	♖xc7	♘e5
47	♖xb7	♘xc4
48	b3	**Black resigns**

A highly impressive performance by Kasparov, against the British Grandmaster who will challenge for his world title in 1993.

Kasparov is mobbed by autograph-hunters at Baden-Baden 1991 (Helmut Schneider).

GAME TWELVE

White: Gary Kasparov (Russia)
Black: Predrag Nikolic (Bosnia–Herzegovina)
Manila Olympiad 1992
Queen's Gambit Declined, Slav Defence

There is no disguising the fact that the 1992 Manila Olympics were, in the first instance, a triumph for Russia and the numerous states of the former Soviet Union. The top scores were: (1) Russia 39/56; (2) Uzbekistan 35; (3) Armenia 34½; (4) USA; (5) Latvia; (6) Iceland; (7) Croatia; (8) Georgia; (9) Ukraine; (10) England. The outstanding individual performance of the entire competition was that of Kasparov himself, who scored an unbeaten eight and a half points out of ten on top board, thus proving a superb inspiration for his team mates. Kasparov's gold-medal winning performance was not just impressive from a sporting point of view, but also replete with the kind of attractive attacks which have made his games so appealing to a wide public.

1	d4	d5
2	c4	c6
3	♘c3	

Inviting the sharp Winawer Counter-Gambit of the Slav Defence, which has become quite popular in recent tournaments.

3	...	e5
4	dxe5	d4
5	♘e4	♕a5+ *(64)*
6	♗d2	

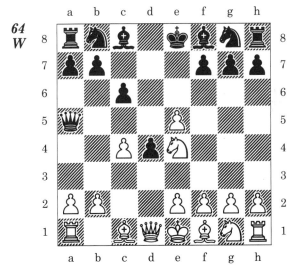

64
W

6 ♘d2 was tried twice at Linares 1992: 6 ... ♘d7 7 e6 fxe6 8 g3 e5 was Karpov–Bareev; while 6 ... ♘h6 7 ♘gf3 ♘f5 8 g3 was Beliavsky–Gelfand. Kasparov tries an altogether different approach.

6	...	♕xe5
7	♘g3	♕d6

Beginners' texts frequently inveigh against early moves of the queen, to the detriment of mobilising the other pieces. Here Nikolic has clearly broken that rule but seems, in any case, to stand reasonably well. His pawn on d4 exerts a cramping effect on the white position and, meanwhile, Black can look forward to a free development of his remaining units.

8	♘f3	♘f6
9	♕c2	♗e7
10	0-0-0	0-0
11	e3	dxe3
12	fxe3!	(65)

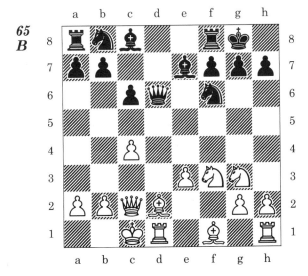

A brilliant decision by the champion, and one which shows that he places dynamic attacking considerations before all thoughts of strategic caution. Most players here would have chosen the risk-free recapture 12 ♗xe3, when with the symmetrical pawn structure the game would probably have burnt out to a draw. Kasparov, on the other hand, is happy to

accept a weak isolated pawn on e3 in order to transfer his queen's bishop to an attacking post on the long dark-squared diagonal.

| 12 | ... | ♕c7 |
| 13 | ♗c3 | |

A key move in the white set-up. The position of this bishop, aiming directly at the black king, is absolutely critical for the further course of the game.

13	...	♗g4
14	♗d3	♘bd7
15	♗f5	♗xf5
16	♘xf5	♖fe8
17	♘xg7!!	(66)

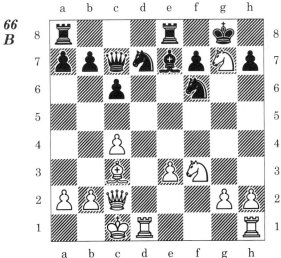

A superbly elegant sacrifice which wrenches Black's king directly into the firing line of White's dangerous bishop.

17	...	♔xg7
18	♕f5	♘f8
19	h4	h6
20	g4	

Now White's plan becomes perfectly clear. The inexorable advance of the white g-pawn will be instrumental in regaining the lost material.

| 20 | ... | ♕c8 |

Grandmaster Predrag Nikolic, one of the most consistent players in the world (Mark Huba).

Nikolic defends himself as best he can, but even the exchange of queens cannot permanently diminish the force of White's attack.

21	♕xc8	♖axc8
22	g5	♘h7
23	e4	♖cd8
24	♖df1	♔f8
25	gxf6	♗xf6
26	e5 *(67)*	

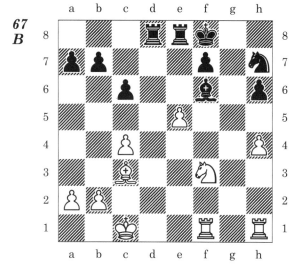

67 B

Material equilibrium has been re-established, but Black's pieces have been driven back and White enjoys pressure in all parts of the board.

26	...	♗g7
27	♖hg1	c5
28	♔c2	♖e6
29	♖g4	♗h8
30	b4!	

Cleverly opening a second front so that White can penetrate the black camp through the soon-to-be-opened b-file.

30	...	b6
31	bxc5	bxc5
32	♖b1	♖a6
33	♖b2	♗g7
34	♖b7 *(68)*	

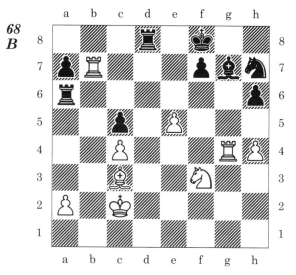

68 B

Sacrificing a pawn to inaugurate the final assault.

34	...	♖xa2+
35	♔b3	♖a6
36	e6	

A brilliant concluding coup which terminates Black's resistance, for if 36 ... ♗xc3 37 ♖xf7+ forces checkmate in short order.

| 36 | ... | ♖xe6 |
| 37 | ♖xg7 | **Black resigns** |

A wonderfully energetic and vibrant game by the World Champion. This game won the gold medal for the single most brilliant win of the entire Manila Olympics!

62

Gary Kasparov in profile (Mark Huba).